PET CARE LIBRARY

Caring for Your Cat

by Derek Zobel

BELLWETHER MEDIA · MINNEAPOLIS, MN

Note to Librarians, Teachers, and Parents:

Blastoff! Readers are carefully developed by literacy experts and combine standards-based content with developmentally appropriate text.

Level 1 provides the most support through repetition of high-frequency words, light text, predictable sentence patterns, and strong visual support.

Level 2 offers early readers a bit more challenge through varied simple sentences, increased text load, and less repetition of high-frequency words.

Level 3 advances early-fluent readers toward fluency through increased text and concept load, less reliance on visuals, longer sentences, and more literary language.

Level 4 builds reading stamina by providing more text per page, increased use of punctuation, greater variation in sentence patterns, and increasingly challenging vocabulary.

Level 5 encourages children to move from "learning to read" to "reading to learn" by providing even more text, varied writing styles, and less familiar topics.

Whichever book is right for your reader, Blastoff! Readers are the perfect books to build confidence and encourage a love of reading that will last a lifetime!

This edition first published in 2011 by Bellwether Media, Inc.

No part of this publication may be reproduced in whole or in part without written permission of the publisher. For information regarding permission, write to Bellwether Media, Inc., Attention: Permissions Department, 5357 Penn Avenue South, Minneapolis, MN 55419.

Library of Congress Cataloging-in-Publication Data

Zobel, Derek, 1983-
Caring for your cat / by Derek Zobel.
   p. cm. – (Blastoff! readers. Pet care library)
Summary: "Developed by literacy experts for students in grades two through five, this title provides readers with basic information for taking care of cats"–Provided by publisher.
 Includes bibliographical references and index.
ISBN 978-1-60014-465-3 (hardcover : alk. paper)
1. Cats–Juvenile literature. I. Title.
SF445.7.Z63 2010
636.8–dc22   2010011408

Text copyright © 2011 by Bellwether Media, Inc. BLASTOFF! READERS and associated logos are trademarks and/or registered trademarks of Bellwether Media, Inc.

Printed in the United States of America, North Mankato, MN.
080110   1162

Contents

Choosing a Cat

Thousands of years ago, the ancient Egyptians kept cats as pets. They believed the cats brought them good luck. Today, millions of people keep cats as pets.

Before you bring a cat into your home, be sure you are ready to care for a pet. Cats can live for more than 15 years. Your pet cat will need your attention every day of its life.

Sphynx

Ragdoll

Maine Coon

Cats come in many different shapes, sizes, and colors. There are about 40 cat **breeds**. They have different appearances and behaviors. It is important to consider all of these characteristics when selecting your cat.

Siberian

Breeds vary in intelligence and personality. Some breeds are very friendly, while others like to be alone. If you have other pets, it is important to choose a breed that will get along with them.

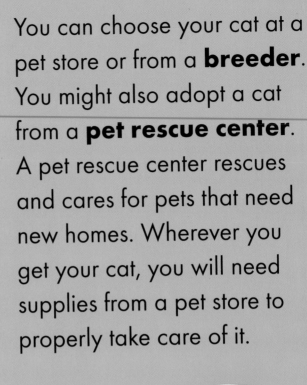

You can choose your cat at a pet store or from a **breeder**. You might also adopt a cat from a **pet rescue center**. A pet rescue center rescues and cares for pets that need new homes. Wherever you get your cat, you will need supplies from a pet store to properly take care of it.

food bowl

Supply List

Here is a list of supplies you will need to take care of a cat.

- litter box and scoop
- cat litter
- cat food
- cat toys
- scratching post
- food and water bowls
- grooming brush
- cat carrier

scratching post

cat toys

Your Cat at Home

A cat can have trouble adjusting to a new home. When you bring your cat home, it might run and hide. You can help your cat by making it feel safe. Bring your cat to a quiet part of your house where it can rest.

Put a **litter box**, food, water, and some toys by your cat. Let your cat explore your home for a few days. It will soon get comfortable with its new surroundings and the people and pets in your home.

Care Tip

You will need to scoop dirty litter out of your cat's litter box every day. Replace all of the cat litter in the box every couple of weeks.

litter box

Feeding Your Cat

Care Tip

Growing kittens need special food with extra protein and fat. They should be fed three times a day.

Cats are **carnivores**. Pet stores and grocery stores carry a wide selection of cat food made with meat. Adult cats should be fed twice a day.

Dry cat food will make your cat thirsty. Always leave water out for your cat to drink. For a treat, add some ice cubes to the water.

Cat Behavior

Cats like to be **independent**. Your cat will want time alone to play and explore. It will **groom** itself to keep clean.

Your cat will spend a lot of time sleeping. Many cats sleep about 16 hours a day!

Cats use sounds and their bodies to show how they are feeling. When your cat is relaxed, it will purr and slowly sway its tail. It might also lie down and start to close its eyes.

If your cat is frightened, it will arch its back and its hair will stand up. It might growl or hiss if it gets angry.

scratching post

Toys can help your cat exercise and stay healthy. Cats have a natural urge to scratch. A **scratching post** will keep your cat from scratching your furniture.

Cats also like to **pounce**. Stuffed mice, yarn, and other toys help your cat practice its hunting skills. They also give you and your cat a fun way to play.

Keeping Your Cat Healthy

If you notice your cat is not eating or playing, take it to a **veterinarian**. Your cat should see a veterinarian once a year for a checkup.

The connection you share with your pet cat can be very strong. If you take good care of your cat, you will have a companion for many years.

! fun fact
Some pet cats have lived to be over 35 years old!

Glossary

breeder—a person who raises cats and sells them to other people

breeds—types of cats

carnivores—animals that eat meat

groom—to clean; cats groom themselves by licking their fur.

independent—alone

litter box—a place where a trained cat goes to the bathroom

pet rescue center—a place that rescues pets; pet rescue centers care for pets until new owners can be found.

pounce—to jump on; cats have a natural instinct to pounce; they enjoy pouncing on toys, and also on small animals when they are hunting.

scratching post—a post that cats enjoy scratching; cats have a natural instinct to scratch; scratching keeps a cat's claws clean and short.

veterinarian—a doctor who takes care of animals

To Learn More

AT THE LIBRARY

Landau, Elaine. *Your Pet Cat*. New York, N.Y.: Children's Press, 2007.

Ring, Susan. *Caring for Your Cat*. New York, N.Y.: Weigl Publishers, 2003.

Stevens, Kathryn. *Cats*. Mankato, Minn.: The Child's World, 2009.

ON THE WEB

Learning more about pet care is as easy as 1, 2, 3.

1. Go to www.factsurfer.com.

2. Enter "pet care" into the search box.

3. Click the "Surf" button and you will see a list of related Web sites.

With factsurfer.com, finding more information is just a click away.

Index

The images in this book are reproduced through the courtesy of: Eric Isselée, front cover; Ostanina Ekaterina, front cover (small), p. 21 (small); Juniors Bildarchiv/Photolibrary, pp. 4-5, 11 (small), 15, 18; Linn Currie, p. 6 (top, middle, bottom); Elena Leonova, pp. 6-7; Comstock/Photolibrary, pp. 8-9; Eric Le Francais, p. 9 (top); Adam Edwards, p. 9 (middle); Juan Martinez, p. 9 (bottom); Michal Bednarek, p. 10; Juniors Bildarchiv/Age Fotostock, pp. 11, 13 (small); Steve Lyne/Getty Images, pp. 12-13; Martin Smith, p. 14; Konrad Wothe/Photolibrary, p. 16 (small); Bartlomiej Nowak, pp. 16-17; Wildroze, p. 19; Monkey Business Images, pp. 20-21.